AF254926

THIS BOOK BELONGS TO

....

For further information contact
Dayane, d.dorlys@gmail.com
ISBN 978-1-9169065-0-1
Made in England

FOLLOW US
ON OUR SOCIAL NETWORKS

@Little_Dayane

To Little Dayane
the girl I once was
and to you, the beautiful girl
reading this book.

May you never forget
all the beautiful words
of the Magic Mirror.

The Magic Mirror is the voice
of many truths
that we often tend to forget.

Remember, you are more
than a child.
You are
the future of our kind!

To you, the caring reading partner.

Thank you for taking part in this bedtime adventure
full of beautiful reminders of our self-discovery.

To all my supporters, thank you for being important
members of "**Little Dayane's Foundation.**"
A movement of change for a better future.

Dayane Dorlys
Haitian-born French Author

"I am on a mission to help young people on their journey of self-discovery.
I use my writing as an educational tool to promote inner beauty and strength.

Children need to know their value and to learn how to love themselves
just the way they are.

I write motivational bedtime stories because that special moment before bedtime
is perfect for inserting positive messages of self-love
and boosting our little ones' self-esteem.

Children are the future of our world in all shapes, shades and sizes."

THE MAGIC MIRROR

Little Dayane's Mummy had a magic mirror.

Little Dayane always wondered what special powers the mirror had.
One night, at bedtime, her Mummy decided it was time to show Little Dayane the
magic of the mirror.

Beauty Of My Hair
You Are Amazing

Mummy sat on the bed and tucked in Little Dayane.

"When I was a little girl just like you, many people told me unkind things about
myself that were not true.
So, one night I wished with all might to be able to hear the truth.
When I woke up I saw a beautiful shiny mirror on my bed.
I asked myself, how did that mirror get there?
Suddenly, I heard a voice reply."

"The answer is in your heart."

Little Dayane was very excited.

She wanted to hear the voice, just like her mum.

"Hold on, Little Dayane," said her mum.
"Before you can use the power of the magic mirror, the mirror has to choose you."

Beauty
Of My
Hair
You
Are
Amazing

Beauty
Of My
Hair
You
Are
Amazing

Little Dayane started to feel a little bit sad.
"What if it doesn't choose me, Mummy?" She asked.

"There is one thing you need to know before you get started", Mummy said with a smile.

"What is it, Mummy?" Little Dayane asked excitedly.

"You need to know who you are."

"I know that already!" Smiled Little Dayane. "I'm a little girl."
But just then, there was a tinkling sound.

"Ssshhh," Mummy said gently.
"The mirror is talking to me. It's telling me that you are more than just a little girl.
You are the future of my kind."

"Really, Mummy? I am?" She asked.

The mirror whispered.

"Of course,
the answer
is in your heart."

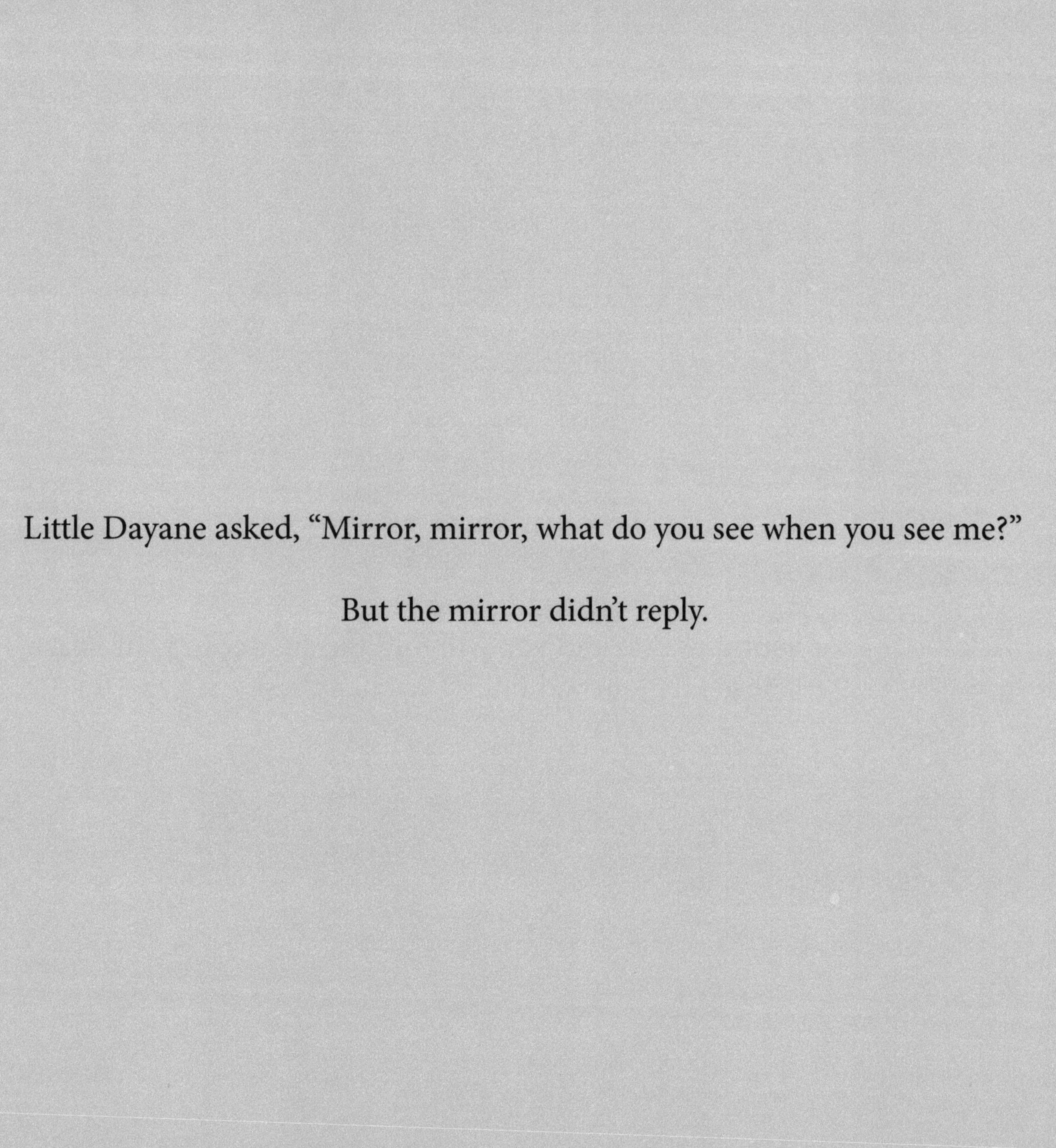
Little Dayane asked, "Mirror, mirror, what do you see when you see me?"

But the mirror didn't reply.

"I don't think the mirror chose me, Mummy." She said disappointedly.

Her mum said,
"Ask the mirror your question and you will find the answer in your heart."
She gently touched Little Dayane's chest.

Beauty
Of My
Hair

You
Are
Amazing

Beauty
Of My
Hair
You
Are
Amazing

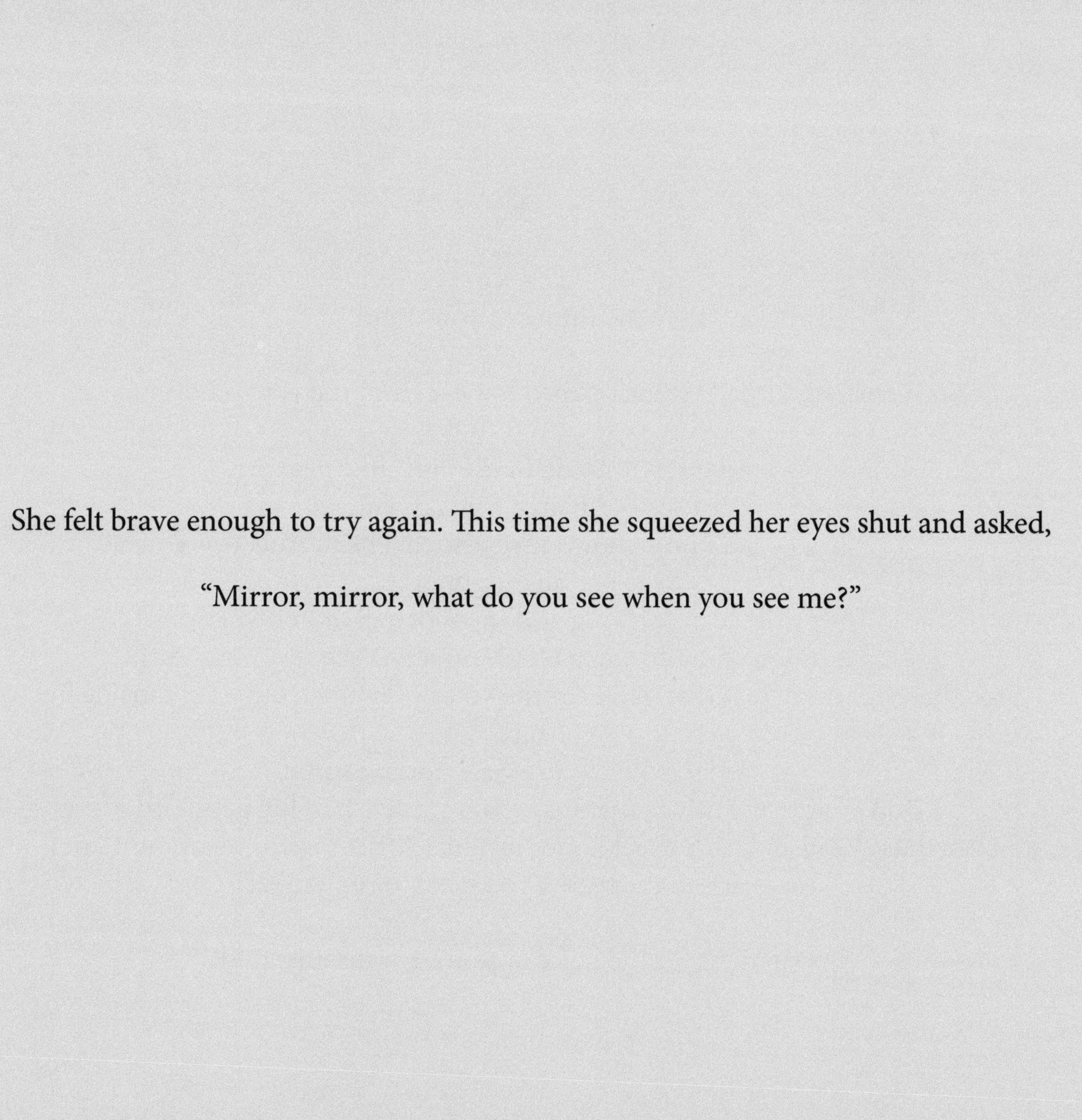

She felt brave enough to try again. This time she squeezed her eyes shut and asked,

"Mirror, mirror, what do you see when you see me?"

"I see the future of your kind."

So surprised, Little Dayane opened her eyes and the voice continued.

"I see a girl with radiant skin just like pearls.
I see her hair, a true crown.
Only a queen knows how to wear such a beautiful crown.
I see her big bright eyes.
They will see everything and show her all of her worth.
I see her unique nose to smell all the amazing scents of the world.
I see those fantastic ears that will hear the voice of many truths, kept inside her heart.
I see large lips to draw a stunning smile.
Don't forget the things that make you smile when life gets hard.
I see those beautiful high cheekbones just like Africa's stunning mountains.
These are all the truths you need to remember."

As suddenly as the voice appeared, it disappeared.

"Mummy, the mirror chose me and told me
all of these wonderful things."

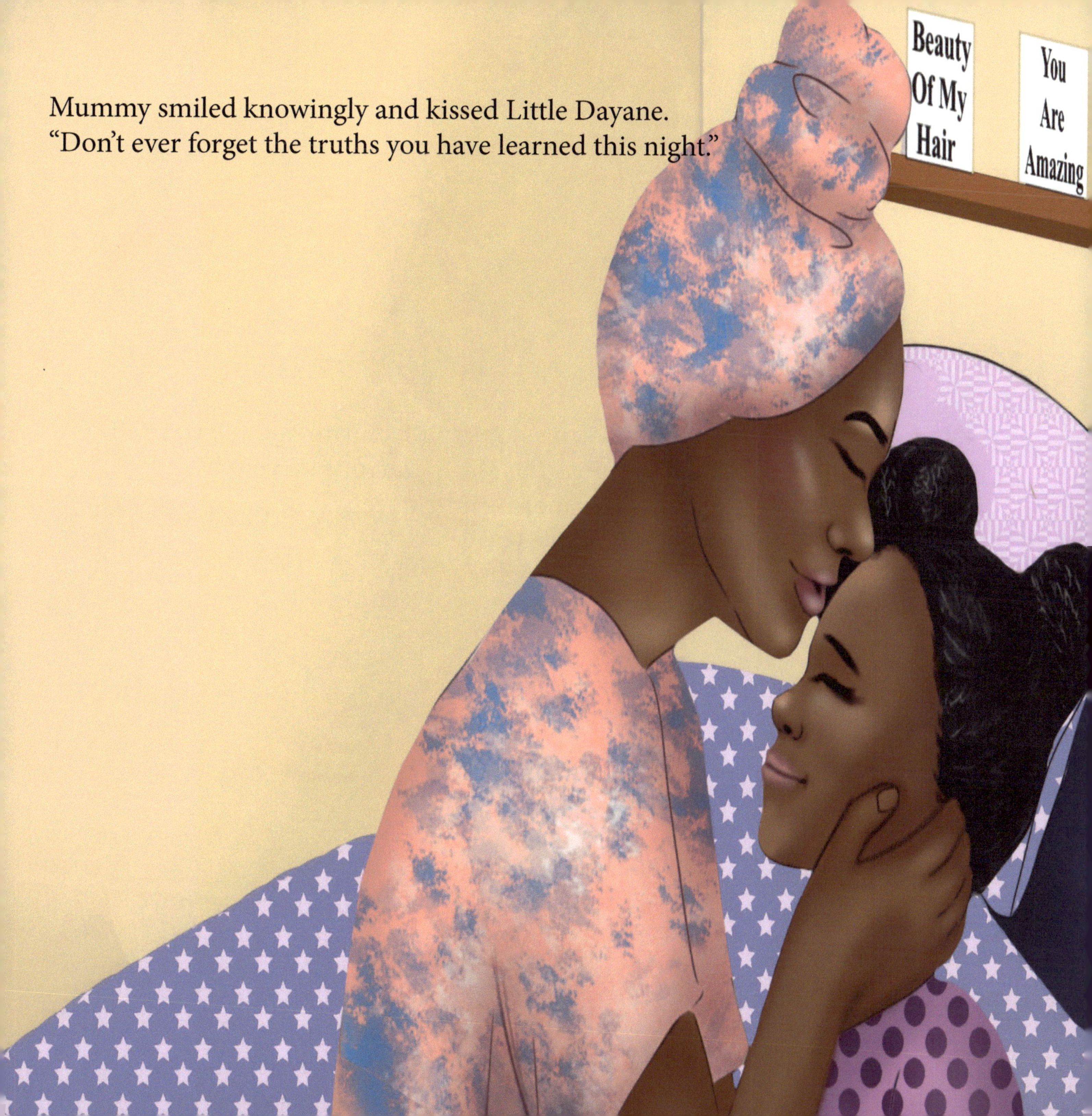

Mummy smiled knowingly and kissed Little Dayane.
"Don't ever forget the truths you have learned this night."

"If you ever need to be reminded, just look in the mirror and tell yourself
all of the beautiful things the Magic Mirror told you.
My Little Dayane, my little queen.
I love you.
Goodnight."

Do you remember what the magic mirror said to Little Dayane?

What do you think will happen when Little Dayane wakes up in the morning?

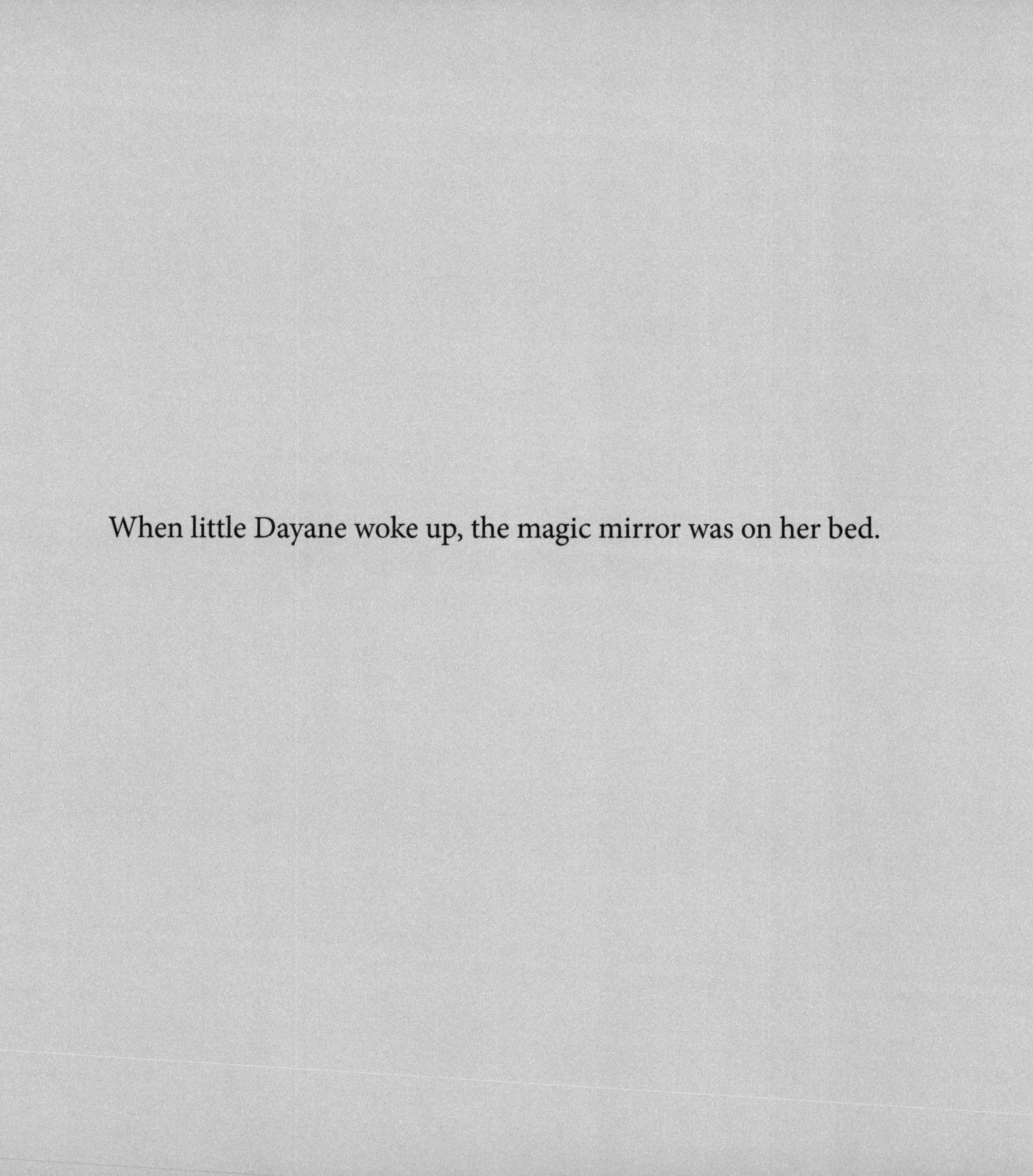

When little Dayane woke up, the magic mirror was on her bed.

She went into her mum's room and said,
"Mummy, you left your mirror on my bed."

Her mum shook her head and smiled,
"No, my mirror is in its place." She pointed to the mirror on her dressing table.

Little Dayane went back into her bedroom. She now had her very own mirror.
She smiled.
"I wished for the truth, and now I know it was always in my heart."

THE END

Draw yourself

Draw your reading partner

You are ...

BEAUTIFUL

STRONG

POWERFUL

A QUEEN

Find the missing letters

I AM B ... A ...T ... F ... L.

I AM ... T ... O ... G.

I A ... P O ... E ...F ... L.

... AM A Q ... E E ...

Write a motivational message for your child.

Signature